Helping Children See Jesus

ISBN: 978-1-64104-043-3

REPENTANCE
A Changed Mind, Heart and Will
New Testament Volume 6: Life of Christ Part 6

Author: Ruth B. Greiner
Illustrator: Frances H. Hertzler
Computer Graphic Artist: Jonathan Ober
Typesetting and Layout: Patricia Pope

© 2018 Bible Visuals International
PO Box 153, Akron, PA 17501-0153
Phone: (717) 859-1131
www.biblevisuals.org

All rights reserved. No part of this publication may be reproduced, stored in a retrieval system or transmitted in any form by any means, electronic, mechanical, photocopy, recording or otherwise, without the prior permission of the publisher, except as provided by USA copyright law.

RELATED ITEMS

To access related items (such as activities, memory verse posters and translated texts) please visit our web store at shop.biblevisuals.org and enter 1006 in the search box on the page.

FREE TEXT DOWNLOAD

To access a FREE printable copy of the teaching text (PDF format) in English or other available languages, enter S1006DL in the search box. Add the item to your cart, and use coupon code XTACSV17 at checkout. Once your order is processed you will receive an email with a link to the free download.

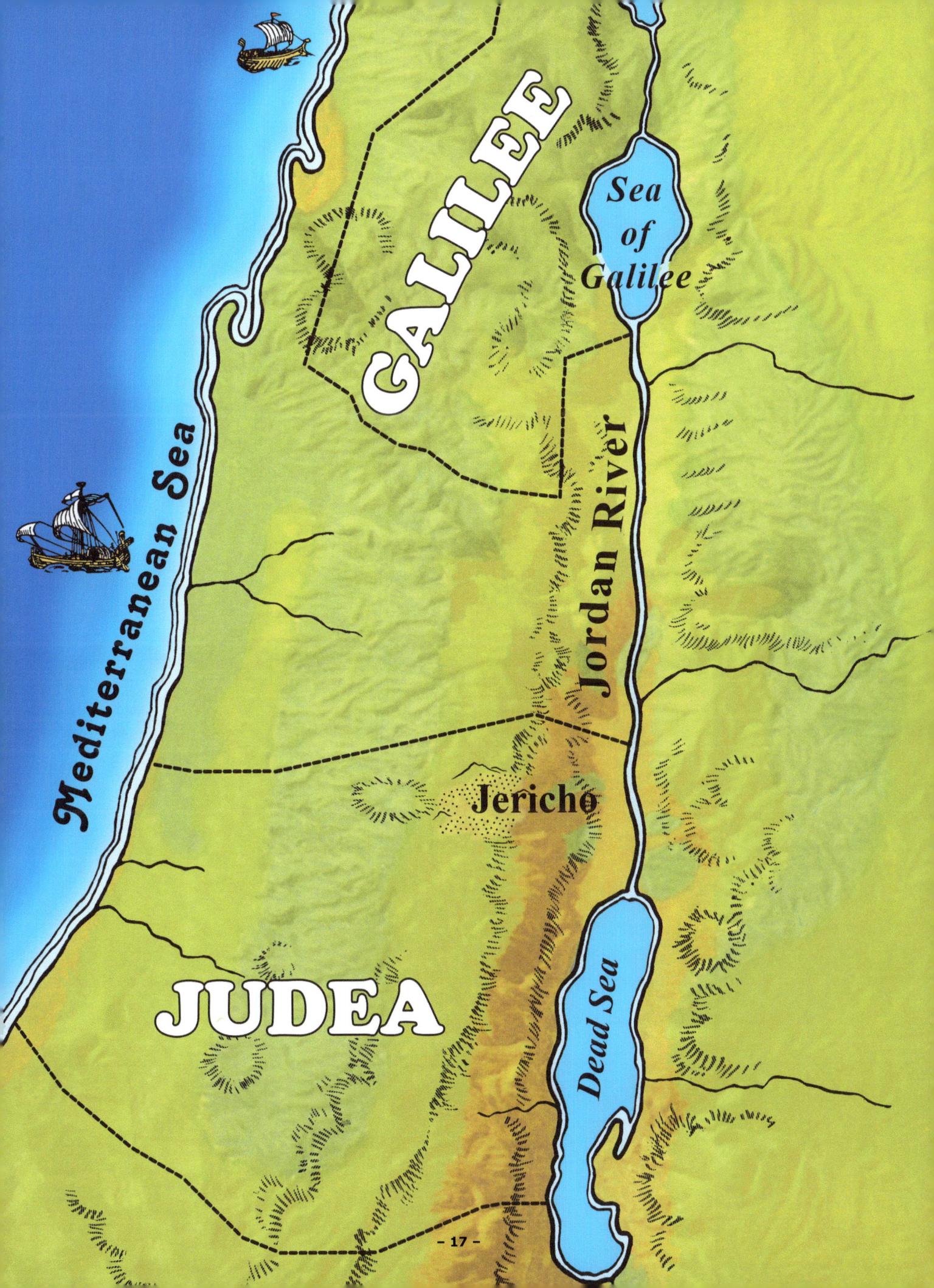

Repentance

heart and will!

change of mind,

God

sin

"I say unto you, that . . . joy shall be in Heaven over one sinner that repenteth."

Luke 15:7a

Lesson 1
ZACCHAEUS

NOTE TO THE TEACHER

In order to avoid confusion, we must know the exact meaning of Bible words. This is especially true with regard to the word *repentance*.

When one repents, it means he has had *a change of mind*. That change of mind affects:

(1) His thoughts (that is, his intellect)
(2) His heart (his desires)
(3) His will (his actions)

So that you will remember that repentance means to change the mind, it would be well to remember two verses that clearly reveal the meaning. Matthew 21:28, 29: "But what think ye? A certain man had two sons; and he came to the first and said, 'Son, go work today in my vineyard.' He (the son) answered and said, 'I will not.' But afterward he repented and went."

That is precisely the meaning of the Bible word *repent*. The son changed his mind. First, his thoughts were changed. He had thought that he would not go to work in the vineyard. His heart, however, told him that he was doing wrong by refusing to obey his father. So, after his thoughts and desires were changed, his will was changed. And when his will was changed, he went to the vineyard. He had *repented*.

In our last series of lessons we studied *faith*. We learned that in order to be born again into the family of God, we must believe that the Lord Jesus is the Son of God and that He died for our sins. The person who believes these truths is said to have *faith*. But how did he get that faith? God gave it to him!

Just as a person exercises faith at the moment of the new birth, so he exercises *repentance* [a change of mind] at the moment of the new birth. Repentance is included in believing and cannot be separated from it. The Holy Spirit of God reveals to man that he is a sinner in rebellion against God, and that he is evil in nature. So man repents because God has gone before, showing that man what he is. Like faith, repentance is a gift of God.

It must be remembered that salvation is *all* of God. Christ Jesus died in our place. God, by the power of His Holy Spirit, gives us faith to believe in the Lord Jesus and to receive Him. And that same Holy Spirit is the One who causes us, at the moment of believing, to repent (have a change of mind, heart and actions).

Scripture to be studied: Luke 19:1-10

The *aim* of the lesson: To show that Zacchaeus truly believed in the Lord Jesus and received Him as his Saviour. This is proved by the fact that he repented (turned from his sin).

What your students should *know*: That Zacchaeus became a happy man when he turned to Jesus and away from his proud, self-centered life.

What your students should *feel*: A deep desire to turn *to Christ* and away *from sin*.

What your students should *do*:
Unsaved: Believe in the Lord Jesus Christ and turn from his/her sin.
Saved: Show friends and family how they can turn to Christ.

Lesson outline (for the teacher's and students' notebooks):

1. A desire to see Jesus (Luke 19:1-3).
2. Meeting Jesus (Luke 19:4-6).
3. Repenting of sin (Luke 19:7).
4. Proof of repentance (Luke 19:8-10).

The verse to be memorized:

The Lord Jesus said, "I say unto you, that . . . joy shall be in Heaven over one sinner that repenteth." (Luke 15:7)

THE LESSON

Heaven is a happy place! Our memory verse tells us of something that causes joy in Heaven. What is it? . . . Yes, there is joy when a sinner repents.

In your notebook, after you write the memory verse, you should write this true meaning of the word *repent*:

The Bible word *repent* means *to have a change of mind*.

When one truly believes in the Lord Jesus as Saviour, he turns to Him and away from his sin. Because he chooses Christ instead of his old sinful life, he has had a change of mind. His heart has been changed. His actions have been changed. He has repented.

Listen carefully to the lessons in this series for there is a message for *you*. The unsaved must repent [change the mind]. And there are times when born again believers must also repent.

1. A DESIRE TO SEE JESUS
Luke 19:1-3

Zacchaeus lived in Jericho–a city that was called the "City of Palm Trees." (See Deuteronomy 34:3.) Many people passed through Jericho as they journeyed to and from Jerusalem.

One day Someone very special came to Jericho. Great crowds followed Him. He had been in and around Jericho before. On that occasion He had healed some blind men. (See Matthew 20:29-35; Mark 10:46-52; Luke 18:35-43.) So the people remembered Him and crowded around Him. Everyone wanted to see this Man–the Lord Jesus Christ. People pressed so tightly together that no one could push through to get to the Son of God. Many of the men and women must have wished that they could invite Jesus to their homes so they could talk with Him away from the crowd.

Show Illustration #1

Zacchaeus was at the outside edge of the crowd. He tried and tried to get a look at Jesus. He had heard of the great things Jesus had done. *If only I could see Him!* Zacchaeus wished. But he was not tall enough to see over the heads of the other people. He was probably the shortest man in the crowd.

Poor short Zacchaeus! What should he do? He could not push his way through the throng. The people would not let him through. They knew Zacchaeus. They knew he was rich. And they did not like him. In fact, some hated him! Zacchaeus was the chief collector of taxes. Tax collectors often took more money from the people than they should have taken. They kept the extra money for themselves and became rich. Evidently Zacchaeus had done this. So the people disliked him.

2. MEETING JESUS
Luke 19:4-6

But the short man was not satisfied to be at the edge of the crowd. He wanted to see Jesus! And there seemed to be only one way he could do it. Quickly he ran far ahead of the others to a tree by the side of the road. It was not one of the many palm trees in the city. It was a sycamore tree–a tree with sweet-tasting fruit. But Zacchaeus was not interested in eating the fruit now. Looking up he saw a branch that would be exactly right for his purpose. He stretched for the branches and pulled himself up and up and up.

Show Illustration #2

He balanced himself on one of the big limbs and looked down the road. The multitude was coming closer. Zacchaeus was now high above everyone else. *I will surely be able to see Jesus now,* he thought. *And no one will notice me away up in this tree.*

The crowd came closer and closer. Zacchaeus strained his eyes. There was only One he wanted to see–the Son of God. Then he saw Him. Zacchaeus never took his eyes off Jesus. When Jesus was right under the tree where Zacchaeus was, He stopped.

The crowd stopped as well. Jesus looked up into the tree. Then the crowd looked up.

Show Illustration #3

"Zacchaeus!" Jesus called.

How does He know my name? Zacchaeus wondered. *He has never seen me before. How did He know I was up here?*

"Hurry and come down!" Jesus ordered. "I must stay with you in your home today."

The Lord Jesus saw me! The Lord Jesus spoke to me–Zacchaeus, the tax collector! And He wants to stay in my house!

These must have been the thoughts that raced through his mind as Zacchaeus climbed down. Then, standing before the Lord Jesus, he looked up–up into the nicest, the kindest, the best face he had ever seen.

3. REPENTING OF SIN
Luke 19:7

Show Illustration #4

When the hated tax collector and Jesus went to the home of Zacchaeus, the people exclaimed, "Jesus has gone to be a guest in the house of a sinful man!"

But the grumbling of the outsiders did not bother Zacchaeus. The most important thing to him was that Jesus was with him in his home. He was happy! Well, he was happy that the Lord Jesus was there. But being in the very presence of the holy Son of God also troubled Zacchaeus. He now realized what a wicked sinner he was. He probably thought of all the money he had wrongfully taken from the people. And something happened deep down inside Zacchaeus.

No longer did he think of himself as an important rich man. No longer did he feel that having money was the most important thing in life. No! As Zacchaeus looked into the face of the sinless Son of God, he believed in Him. He recognized how holy God is–and how sinful he, the tax collector, was. And at that moment, as he believed, he repented (changed his mind). He repented of having selfishly taken so much money for himself. He repented of having stolen from the taxpayers. His mind was changed; his heart was changed; his will was changed. How do we know?

4. PROOF OF REPENTANCE
Luke 19:8-10

Immediately Zacchaeus stood and announced (probably for all the crowd to hear): "Lord, I will now give half of my wealth to the poor. And if I have taken anything from anyone, I will now pay him back four times as much as I have taken."

Show Illustration #5

The life of that man was completely changed. Believing in the Lord Jesus, he repented of the wrong things he had done. His repentance [change of mind] was sincere, for he promised to do exactly the opposite of what he had been in the habit of doing. Now he would *give* to people instead of *stealing* from them.

The Lord Jesus declared, "This shows that salvation has come to this house today. For the Son of Man came to seek and to save that which was lost."

What a happy day it was for Zacchaeus when he turned to the holy Son of God–away from his proud, self-centered life. He was happy because his mind was changed, his heart was changed, his actions were changed. He had turned to heavenly riches in Christ Jesus and away from his earthly riches. The same moment in which he believed in the Saviour, he repented.

To believe in the Lord Jesus Christ as Saviour, to repent as Zacchaeus did and to know our sins are forgiven, is worth more than all the money in the world. Have *you* turned to the Saviour? In turning, has your mind been changed? Has your heart been changed? Has your will been changed? If not, you may repent this very moment.

If you have previously turned to the Lord Jesus and away from your sin, have you shown others how they may turn to Him? Tell your friends and family about Zacchaeus. If you tell them prayerfully, the Holy Spirit of God may prepare their hearts so that they, believing in the Son of God, will repent of their sin.

NOTE TO THE TEACHER

By now you are aware of some of the things which are involved in salvation. Faith (believing in the Saviour) is a necessary part of salvation. Repentance (changing mind, desires and will) is actually a part of faith. And all of these–salvation, faith, repentance–are the work of God in the heart of the one who believes.

Lesson 2
THE RICH YOUNG RULER

Scripture to be studied: Matthew 19:16-30; Mark 10:17-31; Luke 18:18-30

The *aim* of the lesson: To prove that even the best law-abiding person (like the rich young ruler) must believe in the Lord Jesus and receive Him as Saviour.

> **What your students should *know*:** That loving God with the whole heart and receiving Christ as Saviour gives one eternal life.
>
> **What your students should *feel*:** Discontent with anything that means more than loving God.
>
> **What your students should *do*:** Give up the things which come between themselves and the Lord.

Lesson outline (for the teacher's and students' notebooks):

1. Desiring eternal life.
2. Listening to Jesus' teaching (Luke 18:16-17).
3. Jesus' command (Matthew 19:16-21; Mark 10:17-21; Luke 18:18-22).
4. Turning from Jesus (Matthew 19:22-26; Mark 10:22-27; Luke 18:23-30).
5. Money instead of God (Matthew 19:27-30; Mark 10:28-31).

The verse to be memorized:

The Lord Jesus said, "I say unto you, that . . . joy shall be in Heaven over one sinner that repenteth." (Luke 15:7)

NOTE TO THE TEACHER

In the last lesson we learned that *repentance* means to have *a change of mind, heart and will*. Zacchaeus truly believed in the Lord Jesus as the Son of God. We know that he repented of his sin, because he immediately did exactly the opposite of what he had done before: instead of keeping money for himself, he gave to the poor half of all that he had. And he repaid those from whom he had stolen, giving them four times as much as he had taken. Not only did he think differently, he acted differently. That is repentance.

In this lesson we have an example of one who did not repent. Instead of turning to God and away from his love of money, he chose to keep his money for himself and forget God.

THE LESSON

In our last lesson we learned that Zacchaeus repented. What does *repentance* mean? *(It means to have a change of mind, heart and actions.)*

How do we know that Zacchaeus repented? *(He immediately gave half of his money to the poor. And he repaid those from whom he had stolen–repaid them four times as much as he had taken from them.)*

Because Zacchaeus had taken money from others, we know, as he did, that he was a sinful man. We understand clearly that a sinful person must turn to the Son of God, believing Him, receiving Him and repenting of his sin. But there are many good people in the world. What about them? Can good people be assured of eternal life in Heaven? Let us listen carefully to the Word of God and learn what God says about this.

1. DESIRING ETERNAL LIFE

When the Lord Jesus was here on earth, there lived a man who was very rich. He was a good man–a ruler. He may have been a prince or a chief.

Show Illustration #6

I suppose that when he spoke, either in the synagogue or elsewhere, everyone listened to what he had to say. They listened, not only because he was a man of authority, but because they thought him to be a good man. They could not know what was in the heart of the man, of course. They could not know whether or not he had kept all ten of the commandments which God had given hundreds of years before. (See Exodus 20:1-17.) Five of those commandments had to do with the way a man thinks about and acts toward God. And no one can know what another person feels in his heart toward God. God alone knows that. (See 1 Samuel 16:7.)

But those who knew the young ruler knew that he kept the commandments which have to do with the way a man thinks about and acts toward other men: do not murder, do not steal, do not lie. These were among the commandments which the young ruler kept. And everyone knew it. So they respected him. They listened to him when he spoke.

There was probably another reason for their listening to him. He was very rich. He doubtless wore the nicest clothing. His home may have been the most beautiful in town. Quite possibly he had many servants. Many must have wished that they could be as rich as this young man. It was believed in those days that a person became rich because of special favor from God. Looking at the rich man, others must have thought, *Surely God is very pleased with him.*

The man himself did the best he knew to obey the Law. He wanted to be certain of getting to Heaven some day. But down deep inside he had questions which troubled him. *Do I really have eternal life?* he wondered. *Will I go to Heaven when I die? Who can tell me how to be certain of life eternal? Who is wise enough to know?*

2. LISTENING TO JESUS' TEACHING
Luke 18:16-17

Then one day the Lord Jesus Christ came to his village. (The name of the village is not mentioned in the Bible. It was on the coast of Judea beyond the Jordan River.) Certainly the ruler must have heard of people who had gone to Jesus with their questions–rich people, poor people, teachers, good people, sinful people.

Show Illustration #7

Possibly he was watching and listening as Jesus blessed the children who were brought to Him. The disciples had tried to turn the children away because they thought Jesus was too busy. But the Lord

– 22 –

Jesus was never too busy to talk to boys and girls. "Let the little children come to Me," He said. "Never send them away. For the Kingdom of God belongs to men who have hearts as trusting as these little children. And anyone who does not have their kind of faith will never get into the Kingdom of God." (See Luke 18:16-17.)

3. JESUS' COMMAND
Matthew 19:16-21; Mark 10:17-21; Luke 18:18-22

After the Lord Jesus had blessed the children and was on His way down the road, the rich young ruler ran after Him.

Show Illustration #8

Kneeling at the feet of Jesus, he asked the question of his heart: "Good Teacher, what good thing shall I do to get eternal life?"

"Do you know what you are saying when you call Me 'good'?" Jesus asked. "There is none good but One, God." By saying this, the Lord Jesus was trying to help the man to know that He–the Lord Jesus–is indeed God–God the Son. The man had called Him "Good Teacher." But the Lord Jesus knew what was in the heart of the man. And He knew that even though the man had used the word "Good" (a title belonging to God), he did not wholly believe in Jesus, the Son of God. "What you are saying with your lips is not what you believe in your heart," was the meaning of the words of Jesus.

Jesus continued, "You know the commandments [laws of God]: Do not kill, do not steal, do not lie, honor your father and mother, love your neighbor as yourself."

"Master, I have obeyed every one of these laws since I was very young," the ruler replied. "What else must I do?"

The man wanted to do something else. He was not perfectly satisfied. Maybe he wanted to do some great thing–give money for building a synagogue, perhaps. If there were some way of using his money to help assure his having eternal life, he wanted to do that thing.

The Lord Jesus loved the man. He, God the Son, knows all things. He knew what was deep inside the heart of the man. Speaking kindly He said, "You lack one thing. Go, sell all that you have. Give your money to the poor. Then you will have treasure in Heaven. Take up your cross and follow Me."

What is He saying I must do to have eternal life? One thought must have raced after another through the mind of the rich man. *I must follow the Lord Jesus. I must turn away from my riches. I have to give my money to the poor–all of it! My money! My money!*

The man had *said* that he had kept all the commandments. He *said* that he loved his neighbor as himself. But give all his money to his poor neighbor . . . ?

He had *felt* that he loved God with all his heart and would have declared that he had kept the commandment which says, "Thou shalt have no other gods before Me." But to turn to follow God the Son, giving up his money . . . !

He did not understand that in the mind of the Lord Jesus, giving what he had to the poor (the hungry, the thirsty, the naked, the sick), is really giving to Him. (Read Matthew 25:34-40.)

If I am to follow the Lord Jesus, then, like Him, I will not have a nice home. He does not have a home–not even a place to lay His head! (See Matthew 8:20.)

4. TURNING FROM JESUS
Matthew 19:22-26; Mark 10:22-27; Luke 18:23-30

Show Illustration #9

Sadly, the rich young ruler walked away from Jesus, for, the Bible tells us, "he had great possessions." His money was his god!

Turning to His disciples, Jesus said, "How difficult it is for rich people to get into the Kingdom of God! It is easier for a camel to go through the eye of a needle than for a rich man to enter the Kingdom of God."

Since a camel can't go through the eye of a needle, the disciples decided that a rich man could never be saved. But the Lord Jesus settled that problem when He said, "With men it is impossible, but not with God: for with God all things are possible."

Zacchaeus was a rich man. *He* had become a child of God. What was the difference between him and the rich young ruler?

Zacchaeus had turned to God the Son, away from his riches. He had believed on Him. He proved that he had repented [having a change of mind, heart, actions] by giving away half his money and by repaying those from whom he had stolen.

5. MONEY INSTEAD OF GOD
Matthew 19:27-30; Mark 10:28-31

Show Illustration #10

The rich young ruler did not turn to follow God the Son. He chose to continue loving his money more than God. He chose to keep his money for himself, rather than giving to the poor. He did not obey the Son of God. He did not repent [change his mind].

The disciples had watched that rich man walk away from the Son of God. Peter probably spoke for all the disciples when he said, "Lord, we are not like that man. We have left all–our homes, our loved ones, our work–to follow You. What will be our reward?"

Even the disciples were interested in themselves and the rewards that they would receive for following the Son of God.

The Lord Jesus might have rebuked Peter for this. But He, who knows all things, knew what hardships His disciples had suffered. He knew that many of their friends ridiculed them for following the Son of God. Lovingly He promised, "Everyone who has done as you have done–leaving home, brothers, sisters, mother, father, children or property–for love of Me, to tell others the good news, will be repaid many times over in this life as well as receiving eternal life in the age to come."

What encouraging words these were to those men who followed the Lord Jesus!

And the rich young ruler? He had money. That was all. No forgiveness of sin. No promise of being repaid many times over in this life. No eternal life in Heaven. A rich ruler? No! A thousand times no! He was the poorest of the poor. He did not believe in the Lord Jesus. He did not repent. He would not, could not live in Heaven. Poor, poor rich man!

What about you? Have you, by faith, received the Lord Jesus Christ as your Saviour? Have you proved that you have done so by repenting of your sin? (Remember! To repent is to have a change of mind, heart and actions.) If you have not done this, will you do so right now?

Lesson 3
THE PRODIGAL SON

Scripture to be studied: Luke 15:1-2, 11-32

The *aim* of the lesson: To teach Christians that they must repent of any wrong doing if they are to have fellowship with God the Father.

What your students should *know*: God hates any kind of sin.

What your students should *feel*: Conscious of any sin–small or great.

What your students should *do*: Ask God's forgiveness, and, if need be, anyone else he/she has wronged.

Lesson outline (for the teacher's and students' notebooks):

1. A selfish demand (Luke 15:11-13).
2. Selfish living (Luke 15:13-14).
3. Sorrow for selfishness (Luke 15:14-19).
4. Repenting of selfishness (Luke 15:20-24).
5. A selfish brother (Luke 15:25-32).

The verse to be memorized:

The Lord Jesus said, "I say unto you, that . . . joy shall be in Heaven over one sinner that repenteth. (Luke 15:7)

NOTE TO THE TEACHER

Do you know the meaning of the word *prodigal*? A prodigal is one who spends his money wastefully or recklessly.

Study Luke 15:1, 2, 11-32 prayerfully. It is imperative that your students understand that though they be children of God, they may turn away from Him. They are still His children–but are sinful, disobedient children. And as the earthly father of the prodigal forgives his repenting son, so our Heavenly Father forgives us, His born again children, when we repent (change our thoughts, our desires, our actions).

It appears, however, that the Lord Jesus, when He told this parable, was putting the greater emphasis on the older son. It was His answer to the Pharisees and scribes who complained, "This Man receiveth sinners, and eateth with them." The proud, angry older brother who *thought* that he had done no wrong, may have been, in the sight of God, as sinful as his repentant brother.

THE LESSON

In this series we have learned about two men, Zacchaeus and the rich young ruler. Each was faced with the same decision. One believed that the Lord Jesus was the Son of God, received Him as Saviour and repented of his sin. Which one was that? *(Zacchaeus)* How do we know that he repented? *(He began to make right the things he had done wrong. For example, he repaid those from whom he had taken money.)*

How do we know that the rich young ruler did not believe in God the Son? What helps us to understand that he did not repent? *(He refused to follow the Lord Jesus. He chose to keep his money for himself rather than obediently give to the poor.)*

What does the word *repent* mean? *(It means to have a change of mind, heart and will.)*

Zacchaeus and the rich young ruler were unsaved men who met the Lord Jesus. Each had to decide for himself whether or not he would believe in the Saviour. Repenting, you will remember, is a part of believing in the Lord Jesus Christ.

The lesson today has a message for those who have already believed in the Lord Jesus as Saviour. Are there times when born again Christians must repent? Perhaps you are a good Christian. As far as you know, you have not done wrong things. Listen carefully. There may come a time when you may be like either of the brothers in the parable. (A parable is a story of everyday life that is a picture of spiritual truth.)

Here is the parable that Jesus told:

1. A SELFISH DEMAND
Luke 15:11-13

A certain man had two sons. The man must have been very, very rich. He possessed fine jewelry, splendid clothes, good cattle, servants and much more. His sons knew that when their father died, everything that was his would be theirs. They probably did not wish for him to die. But I rather suspect that there were times when they thought about how they would live when the riches of their father would be theirs. Day after day as they worked in the fields, they thought of things they would like to do–if they had the money.

Show Illustration #11

Finally the younger son made a decision. He didn't want to wait until his father died. He wanted his money right now! Boldly he demanded, "Father, give me the portion of goods that will come to me."

Imagine that! He didn't even say, "Please may I have the money?" He fearlessly ordered his father to do something that no father ever had to do.

And do you know what his father did? Right then and there he divided everything he had between his two sons. He did. He really, truly did!

Do you suppose that son was content then to stay at home and work in the field? He was not! A few days later, he gathered everything he had and started the long trip to a country far away. Like most young people, he wanted to go places and see things! And he wanted to be so far away that his father would not know where he was or what he was doing. *No one is going to tell me what I should do or what I cannot do!* he decided. *I will spend my money however I choose. And I will go with whatever friends I please.* He did not care how his leaving affected his father. He thought of only one person: himself. He had his money. He was doing what he pleased. Nothing else mattered.

– 24 –

2. SELFISH LIVING
Luke 15:13-14

Finally he got to the faraway country. He went to all the places he wanted to go.

Show Illustration #12

At each place, he always introduced himself. He treated his new friends to food and drinks. Soon it became known that he had money–lots of money. So he made more friends–and yet more. He had men friends. He had women friends. Fun! That is what the young man had. Everyone was glad to know him. Why? Because he had money. And he spent it freely! Wherever he went people received him gladly.

Then one day he reached for more money. But it was gone! Every last coin was gone! He would have to borrow from his friends. He would have to go to work. His money was gone!

3. SORROW FOR SELFISHNESS
Luke 15:14-19

Strangely, not one of his new friends cared. They wouldn't give him anything to eat. And, worst of all, there was a famine in that land. There had been no rain, so the crops hadn't grown. He went from one place to another trying to get work. Finally a farmer said he would let him work–feeding the pigs. Feeding pigs! The Jewish law in Leviticus said that pigs weren't clean. And so, no Jewish person would ever own them, and certainly would not take care of them. But he was hungry. His clothes were gone. His friends were gone. So he took care of the pigs. Even so, because of the famine, there wasn't enough food for him to eat. And he was hungry! *These pigs are eating better than I am,* he thought. *I wish I could eat some of their food!*

Show Illustration #13

Then he thought about home. He thought about his father. Suddenly, coming to his senses, he exclaimed, "There is no famine in our country! All of the servants of my father have more bread than they can eat. And here am I, starving to death! I will go home to my father and say to him, 'Father, I have sinned against God and against you. I do not deserve to be called your son. Let me be one of your servants!' "

4. REPENTING OF SELFISHNESS
Luke 15:20-24

And he started home. *What will my father say?* he wondered. *Will he let me come back? Will he let me be his servant?* On and on he walked. *What will Father think when he sees me looking like this? Oh, if only I had not lived so selfishly. If only I had not been so sinful. How foolish I have been!*

The mind of that son was completely changed. His heart was changed. His actions were changed. He had repented!

Nearing his home town, a dreadful fear filled him. *What will Father do to me?* he wondered.

When he was yet a great way off he saw someone running toward him. It was his father!

Show Illustration #14

His father threw his arms around his son and kissed him. *My father is kissing me–me, his dirty, smelly, worthless son!*

"Father," he exclaimed, "I have sinned against God and against you! I do not deserve to be called your son anymore."

His father did not let him finish. Instead, he called his servants. "Hurry!" he commanded. "Bring the best robe and put it on him. Put a ring on his finger and shoes on his feet." The son knew what that meant. He was being accepted as a son, not as a servant, for shoes were not for servants.

His father continued, "Go get the fatted calf and kill it. We will have a feast to celebrate. My son whom I thought was dead, is alive. He is not lost. He is found!"

So the feasting began. The father was happy. The servants were happy. And the son was very, very happy.

5. A SELFISH BROTHER
Luke 15:25-32

The older brother had been out in the field when his brother came home. Nearing the house, he heard music and celebrating. He called to one of the servants, "What's going on?"

"Your brother is home and your father has killed the fatted calf to celebrate. Your brother is safe!"

Show Illustration #15

"What! That sinful brother who went off and left all the work for me to do! Now he is home and the calf we have treasured has been made into a feast for that good-for-nothing brother!" Oh, that older brother was angry! He paced back and forth, refusing to go inside.

When his father hurried out to him, the son shouted, "Look! All these years I have worked like a slave for you. Not once did I disobey your orders. And what have you given me? Not even a young goat so I could have a feast for my friends! But your other son wasted all your money doing wicked things. Now, when he comes back home, you kill the best calf for him!" He was not happy that his younger brother had come home. He was not happy that the sinful son had repented.

"My son," his father answered kindly, "you are always at home and everything I have is yours. But we had to have a feast and be happy, for, as far as I knew, your brother was dead. But he is alive. He was lost and now he is found."

And that was the end of the parable that the Lord Jesus told.

Why had He told that particular parable right then? There are two reasons:

(1) He wanted us to know that children of God may sometimes do wrong things–things which are sin in the sight of our Father in Heaven. The younger son had wanted to have his own way instead of doing what his father wanted him to do. Those who have been born again may choose to do what they want to do, rather than doing what God wants them to do. They may do sinful things. But, because they are children of God, if they repent (change their mind, their hearts, their will), and if they confess their sin, He will forgive their sin. (See 1 John 1:9.)

(2) The Lord Jesus told this parable to the Pharisees [strict Jewish religious leaders] and scribes [experts in Jewish law].

These men had complained that the Lord Jesus received sinners–and even ate with them! (Remember that He ate at the home of the sinful Zacchaeus.) So He told the parable to show the proud, self-righteous Pharisees and scribes that they were like the older brother. They thought that they were always right in all that they said and did. Few of them would ever change their minds. Their hearts would not be changed. They would not change their actions. And, though they knew a great deal about the Jewish law and though they proudly did good things, they were sinners in the sight of God–sinners just as much as the older brother in the parable.

Are you a child of God? Are you like either of the sons in the parable? Are you a sinful son–but also a repentant one? Or are you like the son who was quite proud of himself, thinking himself to be far better than others–and unrepentant?

Will you ask the forgiveness of your Heavenly Father, repenting of your wrong thoughts, your wrong feelings, your wrong actions? He waits, this very moment, to forgive you!

Lesson 4
REPENTANCE

Scripture to be studied: All references in text.

The *aim* of the lesson: To show that repentance affects the entire personality. To help your students see that their change of minds, hearts and wills has to do with God, with sin and with self.

What your students should *know*: God loves everyone and desires that each realizes his/her sinfulness and selfishness and turn to God.

What your students should *feel*: Thankful that God has provided a way to come to Him.

What your students should *do*: Repent–change their minds about God, sin, themselves.

Lesson outline (for the teacher's and students' notebooks):

1. God's love provided eternal life for all (John 3:16).
2. Responding to God's love (Luke 19:6-9; Matthew 19:16-22).
3. Christians must sometimes repent (Luke 15:12-21).
4. Repentance–a change of mind.

The verse to be memorized:

The Lord Jesus said, "I say unto you, that . . . joy shall be in Heaven over one sinner that repenteth." (Luke 15:7)

NOTE TO THE TEACHER

Has this series of lessons caused you to study diligently? Has it proved helpful to you? We trust so.

What a refreshing thought it is that salvation is wholly a gift of God! God the Father loved the world and gave His Son. God the Son loved the world. He gave His life, taking upon Himself the punishment for the sins of all who would ever live. The Spirit of God speaks to the hearts of individuals, causing them to believe in the Lord Jesus and receive Him as Saviour. And, at the moment they believe, they repent. That is, they have a change of mind, a change of heart, a change of will. All of this is a part of salvation. And *all* is the gift of God.

If possible, bring a clean box, bag or sack to class. Have it filled with dirty rags. Use it after showing Illustration #8.

THE LESSON

Everything that God does is perfect–absolutely perfect! He loves every man, every woman, every boy, every girl. In turn, He wants their love.

But sin separates people from God. So, instead of loving Him, people turn their backs on Him. They choose to do as they please, caring nothing about the true and living God of Heaven. They have no love for Him–none at all.

Those who do not love God, love sin. Usually their first sins are small enough to be thought unimportant. Their lies, the things they steal, their attitudes are typical of all people everywhere. Later, however, the seemingly little sins become more serious. Finally, they enjoy their sin more than anything else. Only one thing they do not enjoy about sin: that is, getting caught in the act–especially if that act is lying or stealing or murdering, or some such thing.

Although our sins may differ, we are aware that *all* have sinned. *All* have come short of the holiness of God. (See Romans 3:23.) While some may think occasionally of God and others may never think of God, we recognize that we *all* have gone astray and have turned to our own way, refusing to follow God and His way. (See Isaiah 53:6.) If we are honest with ourselves, we have to admit that we think more highly of ourselves than we ought to think. (See Romans 12:3.) Such thinking is, in the sight of God, the sin of pride.

1. GOD'S LOVE PROVIDED ETERNAL LIFE FOR ALL
John 3:16

Because God is perfect, He loves us. He loves us with an everlasting love. (See Jeremiah 31:3.) Even before we were born He knew that we would sin. He knew that we would not love Him. He knew that we would love ourselves. But He loved us–and He loves us now, this moment.

How do we know that God loves us? His written Word declares that, "God so loved the world, that He gave His only begotten Son, that whosoever believeth in Him should not perish, but have everlasting life" (John 3:16). His Word also says that God "will have all men to be saved and to come unto the knowledge of the truth" (1 Timothy 2:4). Referring to children, God says in His Word, "It is not the will of your Father which is in Heaven, that one of these little ones should perish" (Matthew 18:14). Also, we read that God is "not willing that any should perish, but that all should come to repentance" (2 Peter 3:9).

The love gift of God to us is His gift of salvation. He waits to give us His salvation gift. How do we get it? By believing the Lord Jesus Christ to be the Son of God who took the punishment for our sin and receiving Him as our own Saviour. Who gives us the ability to believe? God Himself! (See Romans 12:3; Hebrews 12:2; Galatians 5:22.) And, at the moment we believe, something happens inside us–to every part of us: our thoughts are changed; our hearts are changed; our actions are changed. That change of mind is known as what? *(Repentance)*

2. RESPONDING TO GOD'S LOVE
Luke 19:6-9; Matthew 19:16-22

In our previous lessons we learned about two unsaved men who were faced with the same decision. What was that decision? *(Would they believe in the Lord Jesus Christ as the Son of God?)* Which man did believe in Him? *(Zacchaeus)*

Show Illustration #5

How do we know that Zacchaeus truly believed? He began to make right the things he had done wrong. For example, he repaid those from whom he had stolen–repaid four times as much as he had taken. This proves that he had repented. He had changed his mind about sin. Instead of stealing from the taxpayers, he gave money to them.

Show Illustration #8

Do you remember the story of the rich young ruler who came to the Lord Jesus? He thought his life was clean and good. He was very much like this box which I brought with me today. (Show the box, bag or sack.) It looks nice on the outside. The rich young ruler had tried hard to be good. He felt that he had obeyed the laws of God. He did not lie. He did not steal. He honored his parents. He was a good man, so far as other men could see.

Let us imagine that all of the good things that the rich young ruler did are in this box. What a good-looking box it is! *What a fine man I am!* the ruler may have thought. *But there must be something more that I should do to inherit eternal life.*

Kneeling before Jesus he asked, "Good Teacher, what good thing shall I do to inherit eternal life?"

What do you think? Was there one more thing that he could do to become good enough for Heaven? You and I cannot see through this closed box. We cannot tell what is inside, just as others could not see into the heart of the rich young ruler. But the Lord Jesus could see everything–outside and inside. He, the Son of God, knew everything about the man. What do you suppose the Lord Jesus thought of all the fine things the man had done? Did they seem wonderful to Him? Let us open this box and see. (Have someone come and take the dirty rags from the box.) Look at this! There is nothing but dirty rags. How can that be? What about all the good things the man had done? Were they no better than these dirty rags? No, they were not one bit better. God says that "all our righteousnesses [our good deeds] are as filthy rags" (Isaiah 64:6). That means that we ourselves can never do *anything* good enough to get us to Heaven. The Lord Jesus alone can make us clean and good.

The rich young ruler had thought wrong. He had thought wrong about himself. He had thought that his own good behavior could earn him eternal life. But the Lord Jesus wanted him to know that his good works would not get him into Heaven. Jesus knew that there was one thing the young man loved more than God–that was his money. Jesus wanted him to change his thinking. He would have to change his mind about God–and love Him more than his money. He would have to change his mind about himself. Instead of thinking himself to be good, he would have to realize that he was a sinner. He would have to change his mind about sin and understand that his sin would keep him out of Heaven. He would have to believe that the Lord Jesus Christ alone is without sin. He alone can forgive sin.

Was the rich young ruler willing to follow the Lord Jesus? Did he obey the Lord Jesus by giving his money to the poor? No, he did not. He made his choice between the true and living God and his money god.

Show Illustration #9

Was he happy? No! He went away sorrowful. That he had not believed was proved by the fact that he refused to repent. He did not have a change of mind or heart or actions.

3. CHRISTIANS MUST SOMETIMES REPENT
Luke 15:12-21

Are there times when it is necessary for born again people to repent? Yes, there are such times.

Show Illustration #12

The parable of the prodigal son reminds us of that. Willfully he had gone his own way. He did not care that his going to the far country brought heartache to his father. It did not matter to him that his sinful life disgraced his father.

Happily, there came a day when he came to his senses. He realized he had sinned. And he determined to ask his father to forgive him. He was willing to become a slave to his father–if his father would let him come home. He had truly repented!

Did he have to fall down at the feet of his father and beg forgiveness? Did he have to cry a great deal to soften the heart of his father? Did he have to pray and pray and pray? Did he have to make a long explanation of how sorry he was for having sinned? No! Why not? Because his father had a heart full of love for his son. He knew what a self-willed son he had been.

Before the son had said one word, his father had gathered him into his arms and kissed him. Because he had a father's heart of love, he knew that his sinning son had repented, even before the boy exclaimed, "Father, I have sinned!"

Show Illustration #15

What about the son who had stayed at home? Did he need forgiveness? Yes, he did. He was proud of himself. He was jealous of his brother. He stubbornly refused to forgive his brother. Did he repent? No, apparently he did not. Was he still the child of his father? Yes, he was. Was he a happy son? No! Neither can the child of God who will not repent of his wrongdoing have the gifts of the Spirit of God: love, joy, peace. (See Galatians 5:22.)

4. REPENTANCE–A CHANGE OF MIND

When we first began this series you wrote a memory verse under the title REPENTANCE in your notebook. Then you wrote the meaning of the word repent:

"The Bible word *repent* means *to have a change of mind.*"

By now you have learned that when the mind is changed, the heart is changed and actions are changed.

Show Ilustration 16a

Here in our picture the man is hurrying along the road of life.

Show Illustration 16b

Suddenly in his mind and in his heart he realizes that what he is doing is wrong.

Show Illustration 16c

So, instead of continuing in his own way, his actions are changed. He does exactly the opposite of what he had been doing before.

Draw this illustration in your notebook to help you to remember the true meaning of repentance.

Now write:

1. One who truly repents has a change of *mind* about *God*. He has a change of heart. His actions prove that he chooses the way of God.

2. One who truly repents has a change of *mind* about *sin*. His *heart* hates sin instead of loving it. His *will* is changed so that he no longer practices sin.

3. One who truly repents has a change of *mind* about *himself*. His *heart* is turned to God and away from himself. His *actions* honor his Saviour.

You have this in your notebook. Are these things true in your life?

www.ingramcontent.com/pod-product-compliance
Lightning Source LLC
Chambersburg PA
CBHW060802090426
42736CB00002B/122